S0-BIN-177

Girl Who

Girl Who

Poems by Allison Wilkins

CW Books

© 2014 by Allison Wilkins

Published by CW Books
P.O. Box 541106
Cincinnati, OH 45254-1106

ISBN: 9781625491060
LCCN: 2014951806

Poetry Editor: Kevin Walzer
Business Editor: Lori Jareo

Visit us on the web at readcwbooks.com

Grateful acknowledgment to the following journals and anthologies, in which drafts of these poems first appeared, sometimes under different title:

Bloody Bridge Review: "Jesus, Filed Under Supernatural"
Mason's Road: "Collects Light"
OVS Magazine: "Drinks Terror for Breakfast"
Platte Valley Review: "Collects Crows on the Eve of 30"
STILL: "Companion Plants Basil and Tomatoes"
Sugarmule.com: "Learns to Rebuild"
The Adirondack Review: "Tells Stories to Dogs"
The Nassau Review: "Sees Through"
The Prose Poem Project: "Is Threatened By Flowers"
Tulane Review: "Sculpts a Lion"
Word Riot: "Asks the Scarecrow Twenty Questions"
RiverViews: "Wants New Mythology"

I offer my sincere thanks and gratitude to the Virginia Center for the Creative Arts for its space and beauty, and to Writing Workshops in Greece for the sea and light.

Thank you to Lynchburg College, the University of Nevada Las Vegas, and the University of North Carolina at Greensboro.

Thank you to my gifted teachers and mentors and to the insightful readers of these poems in various stages of their beings: Aliki Barnstone, Carolyn Forche, Michael White, Jennifer Clement, Jim Peterson, Bunny Goodjohn, David Roderick, Adrianne Kalfopoulou, Allison Seay, Laura Long, Lisa Hiton, Lauren Clark, Claire Mcquerry, Christian Detisch, my siren sisters: Lauren Allenye, Samantha Thornhill, and Kathryn Smith.

I also must give thanks to my friend Abayo Animashaun for his devotion to poetry; to Christopher Bakken for his line-slashing wisdom; to Elaina Marie, my favorite UMB; and to Crystal, whose support has been central to my life for longer than I can remember.

Table of Contents

Wants New Mythology..........................11
Wakes to Charm Vowels........................13
Chases Crickets..............................14
Thinks She Knows.............................16
Asks the Scarecrow Twenty Questions..........17
Wishes to Be Something.......................18
Files Jesus Under Supernatural...............19
Sleeps Much Later Than Her Husband
    Everyday..............................21
Wants..22
Inks Her Back................................23
Wishes Her Life Was a Young Adult Novel......25
Sees Through 26
Thinks a River is Peace......................27
Drinks Terror for Breakfast..................28
Is Threatened By Flowers.....................30
Parks in the Employee of the Month Spot......31
Companion Plants Basil and Tomatoes..........32
Dreams (Translated) in Italian 33
Loses Track of Time..........................34
Gardens at Night.............................35
Asks the Chihuahua Ten Questions.............36
Wants to Live Only as Long as She Can
    Remember..............................37
Tells a Tale.................................38
Frecks with Grace............................39
Confuses *Picture* and *Pitcher*.............41
Digests in a Green Kitchen...................42
Cultivates 43

7

Dreams of Babies.. 44

Collects Light.. 45

Sorts Through Music Files.................................. 46

Collects Crows on the Eve of 30 47

Smuggles Tornados... 48

Sees in HD... 49

Tells Stories to Dogs.. 50

Kills Octopus... 51

Practices Brushing Her Teeth with Her Finger....53

Dreams Herself Eve.. 55

Puts Flowers in Her Hair................................... 56

Spins Webs.. 58

Looks for Beauty.. 60

Breathes Icicles and Mint.................................. 61

Takes Communion in the Woods......................62

Contemplates Time and Distance.....................63

Asks the Potted Plant Fifteen Questions.............65

Learns to Rebuild.. 66

Wants to Free Elephants.................................... 68

Makes Her Bed in the Afternoons....................69

Sculpts a Lion... 70

Collects Pebbles.. 72

Finds the Sea Cave... 73

Prepares Her Own Nest..................................... 74

"These weeds are memories of those worser hours."
—Cordelia, *King Lear* (4.7.8)

Wants New Mythology

Her myth begins *coming up from the sea*
and ends with two sparrows in flight. In between,

the narrative will unfold, but not neatly.
And it won't be obvious. There's a long

litany of gods, a token heroine of divine birth.
There will be dancing and chickpeas.

Barrels of white wine. Island moonshine.
After opening *in medias res*,

(the island god *coming up from the sea*)
there follows a long dissertation

on the texture of sand. Then
another about the slight burn

of Greek sun. Then she will skip
to honeysuckle plucked

by an ambiguous hand.
And sea urchins. Rock formations at Sikamia.

She will refuse all battle scenes
and trips to the underworld.

She will make no mention of desire
or music. Yes, she'll leave the final image

alone: two sparrows, side by side in flight
before parting. One heading left, the other right.

Wakes to Charm Vowels

Mornings are the worst,
muscles sore from sleep

and stiffness, eyes crusty,
hair knotted, fan clunking off

rhythm on low speed.
The sheets are warm

as peach skin and gas logs.
But the atmosphere is crisp

and she rises unwillingly,
cracks her back with a twist,

pulls her knees to her chest,
fights the urge to curl

into a rocking ball.
Her mouth, vowel-moist,

as her head inventories
the clock's slow tone.

Chases Crickets

Everyone she's ever

is chirping, wings open,
acoustical sails

loud and quick in the heat.
The kindergarten one

gives her chicken pox
while sharing chocolate milk.

The middle school one
holds her hand during lunch,

draws portraits in charcoal,
pastels, and ink.

The high school one
buys beer and fruity booze,

opens
her car door first.

The college one
screams songs on stage,

feeds her French fries
and gravy.

The husband one
builds garden fences,

mows the grass
in an argyle pattern.

She's always the one
following some distant rubbing

of forewings, listening
for her own call.

Thinks She Knows

Bodies are just bodies:
organs, blood, and juice.

Collections of arms and legs
stitched with tendons and sinews.

Bodies spontaneously combust.
Her body is that kind of thing.

Tangible. Something
he used to touch. A vessel. A utensil.

Enclosure. Fetter.
Something he used to want.

A Roman vase. An ornament.
Stuffed in a box. Cobwebbed.

Now her body makes his
infected, inflamed.

Dyspeptic, carcinogenic, cancerous.
She knows she should be quarantined.

Asks the Scarecrow Twenty Questions

Do you mind the dead crows upside down around
      your head?
Can you fire a gun if you need to?
Are you the bogeyman?
Do you like the color green?
Would you prefer a pumpkin head or a burlap face?
Do you eat wheat or are you gluten-free?
What do you think about dialect?
Do you play nicely with others?
Do you like dark chocolate?
Do you mind when dogs pee?
Does it get hot in May?
How does the rain feel at night?
Do you get lonely in the fields?
Do you know Kuebiko, the one who knows
      everything about the world?
Where are your thumbs?
How do sunflowers make you feel?
When do you sleep?
Do you think in terms of binaries?
Do you really have straw for brains?
What would you do if you heard her scream?

Wishes to Be Something

Because she loves the color gray,
she thinks being a rock could be fun.

Except for erosion, a small loss
every day, and maybe the bugs,

creepy crawlies shimmying underneath.
Because she practices a strong mountain pose,

she thinks being a tree might also be nice,
except for the woodpecker and his red head,

or power saws slicing through her bark.
Or something a little less significant,

she thinks, but she cannot imagine a thing
without purpose. Not the butterfly's spread

wings, nor the empty green bottle whose weight
makes it a book end, nor the wind that blows pollen

across the yard, nor the small cedar chest
which holds her grandmother's rings.

Files Jesus Under Supernatural

Her toes long for the sea.
Tossing salt into the boiling

pasta water makes them curl.
She is happy this morning.

On an espionage trip
to the rival bookstore,

she feels compelled
to file the used books.

What she loves most, she uses:
books, bodies, bathrooms.

Toes are just a small fraction
of life, giving balance, helping

to stand and walk. Without balance
bodies would break and bend,

twist into gnarled suicide
trees. Love is rash, inflamed

across the burning body.
Pier della Vigna smashes his head

against the church wall
as the emperor passes in the street.

Sleeps Much Later Than Her Husband Everyday

Her stomach is empty in the mornings.
Acid bubbles at the back of her throat.

The dog crawls out from under the covers
when he hears the spoon clank on a cereal bowl.

She turns the heat off in March
no matter the degree. Later she will

get up, make a cup of tea, read.
But in the first moments

of the day, she stays still under the covers,
places her hands over her belly,

and begins to count the things
that haunt her sleep.

Wants

She wants one more episode of blood coagulating in
          her cup.
She wants to shoot sparks out of her fingertips.
She wants to shatter like glass.
She wants to cock her head, tilt to him, unnerve him.
She wants to slide her hand between flesh and fabric.
She wants to look at him and see.
She wants what she cannot know.

Inks Her Back

At eighteen, *poetry*
in Sanskrit between her
shoulder blades, blue to lavender
fade. She is serious

about the business of poetry.
She drinks tiny cups of espresso,
slurps long, black
cigarettes, chants fat

syllables. Thoughts echo,
jump over other thoughts,
multiply, plural,
until she forgets her point.

At twenty-eight, her lip,
a silver hoop. Her students
whisper. She watches a teeny
spider cross her laptop,

fleeing from the cursor.
She pencils lines through
bad lines, hides dark

chocolate in the closet.

Stands sipping September,
the giant maple
leaves dropping,
braces herself for winter.

Wishes Her Life Was a Young Adult Novel

Knows the protagonist will always
fall in love—true love—except

he will be evil,
but good, like a vampire with a heart

or eyes of gold. And nothing else will happen
because love is the point. But

the vampire is old and traditional.
So the book is a book of manners and behavior.

She puts the book down;
truth is, all she wants is sex.

Sees Through

What she knows is this: he's not fooling anybody
with his fasting and telephone-pole-wrapped car.
He's depressed and uncomfortable being alone, not
okay with the sound of his heart, nor the club mix,
nor the cell phone ringing ringing unanswered, nor
the air leaving his chest at three in the morning. To
help him, she digs a pit for his fear, lures it with the
promise of sunflowers and juniper, skewers it on
bamboo stakes, burns it in crude oil, watches it blaze
a crimson-orange. In the end, she brushes her hands
together, gathers the ash where he falls.

Thinks a River is Peace

It is raining when she closes her eyes
& imagines the current winding tree roots,

tumbling silt. Whenever her toes connect
with water it's wave-pulling magnetic,

diffusing salt where it was fresh,
so little goldfish can pop up from the river

to recline on grassy banks. They digest words
& worms when the sun comes out, at last, to play.

Drinks Terror for Breakfast

Terrified of horses and their size,
afraid hooves would take out an eye,

she would rather guzzle cyanide
than take a pony ride. Spends years

afraid of passing out and puking
in public. Pets a possum by accident

one night while sleeping on a porch swing
with her lover. Its prickled fur not

her cat's fleece. Grows to hate
babies of all shapes and sizes,

except for one Vietnamese
with her soft brown eyes.

Her grandmother gossips
at every meal. She promises

to never slice her wrist
or dangle from a hand-crafted noose,

but booze, sweet booze.
Yes, she sips blood.

Is Threatened By Flowers

She calls the lawn repair man to fertilize the yard.
Then imagines planting basil next to the orange tree,
cross pollination, and spiced tea. There is gum in her
hair and wrens nesting in the gutters. The grass
turns yellow and purple, then periwinkle in the
shade. A frog holds the rain gauge. Phlox crawls.
Deer high jump her fences and eat everything except
for the herbs. The lawn repair man says he has some
bad news. The yard is infested with dandelions and
violets. The dandelions are easy to treat, he says. But
the violets. Those are impossible to kill.

Parks in the Employee of the Month Spot

She didn't earn the title, she just likes the spot. It's under an oak tree near the library. She hauls books and pencils in bins made of burlap and hemp. Gets paid to research obscure poems and forgotten plants. When she was twenty, she worked at a motel. A woman jacked on crack jumped the counter and knifed her in the back. Now she's afraid of things flying towards her face. Blue jays, chalk dust, even a gentle breeze.

Companion Plants Basil and Tomatoes

Baking breads with cinnamon
and packets of yeast, she kneads,
a baker in twilight.

Night dreams of replacements,
counting cigarette butts
littered in conditioned mess.

She stashes fragments
between pages of books
and flosses shoe laces

between blonde braids.
Tending soil with egg shells
and leaves, she plows,

a poet in daylight.
Books heavy and a bag
of organic dirt. She is

the space between
fall and winter, when
the leaves cling branches.

Dreams (Translated) in Italian

The distance wears on her each day
–*mi dispiace per* departing *senza te.*

Patty-caking mothers with smoothing kisses;
couples slurping each other's lips.

She dreams of teaching *poesia*:
knows he will understand the line

break tracing along his neck,
the rhythm of lips iambic

down the spine, the heat of revision.

Loses Track of Time

She is there when language shifts its axis,
tilts toward the abstract. She tries
to calculate a formula for poems,

but keeps arriving at *blue, blue, achoo.*
She finally gives up, decides investment
banking is the way to go. But mergers

& equity destroy management, security,
& soon the world devolves into chaos.
So she gives away everything she owns,

keeps only her skin
& a pair of dark wash jeans.
A squirrel sends her a sweatshirt.

A beetle brushes her hair.
She forages for parsley & mint,
picks strawberries in spring.

Gardens at Night

What she feared as a child:
watermelon seeds in the creases

of her intestines vine
through the alimentary canal.

Now she swallows
cherry pits and hopes they root,

extend beyond the drip line,
tangling ground, branch into

her throat: a cluster of pink and white
blossoming on her tongue.

Asks the Chihuahua Ten Questions

Are you descended from the *Techichi*?
How does the plastic feel against your teeth?
What do you think when you see a squirrel?
If the sweater keeps you warm, why won't you wear it?
Do you prefer the peanut butter or charcoal treats?
How does the grass feel under your paws?
What is it like bury under the blanket in your den?
Is it fun to be from the smallest breed?
What do you see when you look out the window?
Can she be enough?

Wants to Live Only as Long as She Can Remember

She wants to sleep through the night,
wakes up to her grandmother roaming

halls in search of her dead husband,
the dining hall. "They're awfully late

with breakfast," she says. Tomorrow
her grandmother will stare at the TV,

where land is eroding & buildings
collapse over & over into the sea.

Tells a Tale

Her mother's neighbors think that she paints the grass green at night while they are sleeping. That she slips out with a Q-tip and a can of lawn green paint, filling in the lines with paint-by-number design. But really her mother sprays a clear coat of gloss on her artificial turf. Lawnmower doubling as the clever disguise. Lies doubling lies.

Frecks with Grace

At twenty-two she was *so* rock n roll,
so cocaine, *so* loud. Kept her toys

with the old man's secrets
and her childhood dog.

Now she's *so* granola,
with a dash of honey and cinnamon.

She is neither hard nor soft,
will never be an acorn;

she learns her mouth in a river bed,
her toes in a quarry.

She eats large meals in the evening,
knows she should consume more

in the mornings, give calories time
to burn off. Her hair, brown roots,

cracking through the ground.
She wonders if what she has done

today matters. Eventually she puts off sleep
to watch paws running nowhere,

those other two creatures
in bed on their backs.

Confuses *Picture* and *Pitcher*

Her students tease her for the accent
which is sometimes very Jersey
and other times solidly Southern.

In eight years she has tamed it,
made it into a pet, one
that likes to cuddle on the couch

and lick her hands. But every now
and then, something mischievous happens.
The concrete splits open and a violet fog

comes from her mouth. She forgets
to "turn" lights off, instead she "cuts"
at the switch. And she pricks herself with a pen.

Digests in a Green Kitchen

There are blue and yellow ducks all over the walls; a
10-gallon fish tank next to the breadbox where one
beta won't get along with any other fish. A lazy
susan spins 25-pounds of canned beans and
spaghetti sauce in the corner. Brown cabinets so dark
—not even the ceiling fan's light will help her
mother know the secrets baking in the oven. A single
spoon rests inside of a single mug. The timer strains
each second into the sink.

Cultivates

Her grandmother's hands are fat & swollen from
years of assembling radios in a factory line, of
cramming fist to mouth while eating a little of this &
a taste of that. She watches those hands yank at
dandelion weeds and the crabgrass that creeps into
the flower garden. She wants to ask her
grandmother if she knew that somewhere between
the paper mill & farmhouse, he strayed, if there are
more cousins or other uncles, if there is a piece
missing. But while on her knees digging at weeds,
her grandmother smiles, shields small phlox
blossoms, and spreads dark hardwood mulch.

Dreams of Babies

Wet is no longer slick.
Landscaping dries out,
desert, barren,

boards up the gate, rusty nail shut.
A red flood washes through
with each new moon,

but the slick will not come.
The lotus begins to shrivel.
Raisin skin, friction.

She wants the slip back,
lubes doors and alleys,
butters the basements,

polishes oil into any porous surface.
But all the sleek, satiny, smooth
damp and delicious,
cracks bristle, are broken.

Collects Light

Once she was owl eyes,
sharp at night, staring
straight ahead, searching

for prey. But she was not
the owl head rotating
almost upside down,

or the talons, tightly wrapped
around snake scales.
She had no feathers, no

flight. She could blink
and process light. Register
the memory of everything

around her – guide the brain
through woods.
She was the eye—

wide open, eerie yellow.
A witness with no means
to cry out in the dark.

Sorts Through Music Files

Her grandfather was in love with Paula Abdul in the early 90s. This man, who had 3 hard-headed boy children, who drove a tractor trailer for a living, and who read books but never got an education, would flip through the channels hoping to catch MTV playing the video "Two Steps Forward and Two Steps Back" with Paula and Joe Cool the cat, prancing up and down the steps. He'd watch quietly until it was over. Then he'd turn his head to his favorite grand girl child and say, "That is one beautiful woman."

Collects Crows on the Eve of 30

Teaching consumes sleeping.
H1N1 infects her students,
vaporizing them into blue

energy. No bodies
in the classrooms. No bodies
in the air. Sacrificing,

she selects crows
larger than pigs, those that pluck
their black feathers. Gives them

light and antidepressants, rubs
crumbling leaves into their skin.
The neighbors call her a witch.

She sprinkles poems in their yards
at night: a brew of words and rotting
feathers. Her crows turn into dust.

One by one the students
fall from the sky, tattooed
with wings and beaks.

Smuggles Tornados

Her mother prefers flash floods:
mud, the unexpected sound

of rushing water, black mildew
on drywall & baseboards,

the opposite of fire. But she loves
a squall, stands with arms outstretched

while they twist to funnels, waiting
to collect them in her pocket,

hoard their destruction
for another day.

Sees in HD

Everything is so eyelid shut dark, then TV static fuzzy,
before 1080i HD clear. His fingers trace bark
into her vertebrae. His mouth burgeons
leaf buds. He twitters a finch's song
in her ear. When she flutters,
everything is green.

Tells Stories to Dogs

In one there is a glorious bounty of yellow squeaky
balls, in another charcoal treats. Sometimes the Kong
is stuffed of peanut butter, and other times easy
cheese. There are squirrels to chase, leaf piles to
scatter, mud to sniff. There is one about a house
made of chicken jerky and pepperoni treats. In
another, the dog is a doctor; in another a bounty
hunter. Sometimes the dog is a scientist unlocking
the secrets of alchemy. Sometimes the dog must find
the golden bone to destroy the evil witch who cast a
spell over its owner. Sometimes the dogs are
puppies lost in the woods who find their way home
without help from the cat. The dog is always the
hero— leaping fence— saving the helpless girl child
from a speeding train, a poisonous snake, messenger
pigeons, blue cotton candy & rubber boots.

Kills Octopus

Yesterday the butterflies would not stop swarming, fluttering their light around her face and arms. She had no way to ask them what they meant when they landed on her skin.

A gull pulls the entrails from a hedgehog. What can it mean to do such things. Try again anyway, to re-envision the beginning.

At the bottom of the sea, an urchin filters salt through black spines. One giant eye, one sea stone, suctioned to the floor. The constellation of freckles on your left shoulder, he says, encloses my north star, my compass. He will sail forever, he says, for a single golden kiss.

She turns her head. Afternoon light, between pulled curtains, pauses, then looks him in the eye before shattering. He tries to put her back together, but there are too many that will never fit. He pricks his finger against the piece with the darkest shade of blue. This one, she says, she found in the beak of an octopus.

Then, last night, the spider above her pillow,
weaving nightmares, not dreams. Instead of taking
him outside her house, she asked him for
forgiveness, then crushed his body into wall.

Practices Brushing Her Teeth with Her Finger

She looks for him under slices
of chocolate cake drooling raspberry sauce.

When she doesn't find him, she searches
the crowd at a minor league baseball game—

there are poems everywhere, but no him.
She swings a bat, confuses the pitcher,

bunts the ball and stops to buy a hotdog
not because she eats them, but because

this is what you do at a ball game.
She likes the red thread

in the baseball because it's so flossing teeth.
She grabs the total care ADA approved

toothpaste and there he is—tiny, hiding.
But it isn't really him, just a figment

of her imagination or some other reality
where she loves baseball and all the people

are plastic and bristles. When she gives up,
she strolls to the botanical gardens,

stops to smell a blue flower,
finds his face—smiling—in the center.

Dreams Herself Eve

She is there, in the beginning,
for the assigning of labels.

The naming monkey loves her,
gives her all the strong ones

for the trees: Elm, Oak, Willow.
Later they will reclaim them,

cut them down, burn them.
Buildings over the groves.

Even words will smolder then
blow dust through half-open windows.

Puts Flowers in Her Hair

1.

In the spring, it's time for dandelions. She yanks them by the root, braids the flowers into pigtails, and puts the greens in a salad.

2.

In the summer, daisies. She lines them up in a crown, promenades as princess. Bees bomb her head, collecting nectar.

3.

In the fall, magnolia leaves in a bun at the base of her neck. Sometimes adds suet in the middle for cardinals and sparrows.

4.

In winter she picks sprigs of rosemary, places a single stem behind each ear. The herb whispers memories enough to keep her warm under snow and empty trees.

Spins Webs

Next to the stream, broken white wings
morph into a spotted snake. Below a fire

burns as golden hair, through
which a dolphin gasps for air.

Its purple thread of fluke drops
into fat grapes, dangling from vines.

The lion waits, mouth open,
a delicate flower in his teeth.

While she knits her truths in finer threads,
she keeps the last frame blank.

She does not fear the spiders.
She stores them in a jar,

listens to their secrets before
she turns them loose. But if they linger

in the corners of her room,
she wrecks their webs before

weaving their conquered bodies
into fabric birthed from her loom.

Looks for Beauty

She looks for beauty between cans of kidney beans
and again behind honey bees. Looks for
something red with a splash of bone, a dash of green.

But everything she sees is a shade
of yellow or blue. She thinks
she finds beauty hanging on the wall, but

no, it's just a photo of a beach.
A generic shore of generic sand. Again,
on that book cover, where a woman poses

clinging to the chest of a long-haired man.
There, on the side of an abandoned building.
In bricks, forgotten tools, and broken glass.

Breathes Icicles and Mint

This winter, she is beyond hibernation,
beyond death, beyond rebirth.

She layers black leggings
and various college sweatshirts,

makes soups with spinach and pine cones,
pauses to reflect on the future. At one

with cold air and gray, she is squirreling
away, waiting for ground to thaw,

making pyramids of acorns.

Takes Communion in the Woods

She thinks the eating of someone's flesh, the drinking of someone's blood, is too much. In May, she goes into the woods, sprawls out under an oak tree near the bubbling brook, waits for a python to reticulate her. But the python sees that she is good and leaves her alone. So she waits longer. Finally, a copperhead snakes up her body, mistaking it for forest debris, until it sees the flesh of her ankle, plants its teeth.

Contemplates Time and Distance

1.

The little dog sits in her lap
while she addresses letters of protest to Jesus.

She's railing against the injustice
of cockroaches. Constantly evolving,

able to outlast a nuclear bomb.
Such a stubborn existence.

2.

The little dog jumps and barks
at a squirrel in the yard, leaps

through the window,
chases it up a money tree.

As the squirrel jumps from branch
to branch, quarters fall

in rolls of twenty. She collects
them to preserve the seeds.

Asks the Potted Plant Fifteen Questions

Do you get enough light?
Does the dog pee in your pot when no one is looking?
Do you miss the spiders when she brings you back
    inside after it turns cold?
What do you think of frost?
Are you part of the Araceae family?
Do you miss the protection of house on windy
    summer days?
How does the fertilizer taste?
What is it like to purify the air?
Are parts of you toxic?
Do you know that the Greek words *philo* and
    dendron mean "love" and "tree"?
Will you ever stop growing?
Why are you so thirsty?
Do you imagine a bird's nest between your leaves?
Does it bother you to be root bound?
Would you like new dirt?

Learns to Rebuild

She starts to build a renewable house
from broken tree branches and twisty ties.

She finds some earthworms willing
to tunnel into the ground

and a few spiders who drape white
walls. Grass clippings cling

when the wind blows.
Beetles become outlets

she plugs into
to look up words

she doesn't know.
She hangs basil curtains, throws cups

of rainwater at the stones in her path.
Birds circle her old house.

There, she can no longer breathe.
There, she stores destruction,

guarded by black bears
and a swarm of hive-bound bees.

Wants to Free Elephants

She writes: Dear Ring Master,
there will be no more elephants

diving from four story buildings
into tiny buckets of water, no more

women hanging from ropes by their teeth,
no more making fun of the man

with giant feet, no more animal care-takers
working for minimal pay. No more

feeding the goldfish to the canaries,
or frying snickers and twinkies

with funnel cake batter.
There will only be one show

from here on out: the study
of planted seeds and sprouting fig trees.

Makes Her Bed in the Afternoons

She makes a bed of spider eggs,

with a quilt of tomato leaves.

While she naps in the yard,

a queen bee crawls inside her.

The worker drones follow,

building her comb, cell by cell.

Honey, now, oozes from her skin.

Sculpts a Lion

As child, she played with dragons,
stole their fire, replaced it

with florescent tin & a single
apple tree for each charred ember.
She liked to drag her fingernails through

the heat & burn telegraph lines onto her skin.
When she was a teenager, she coveted
the strut of the scorpion, picked it up

by the tail to extract the poison.
She planted daffodils and learned
to read cardiac rhythms.

Now, adult,
she sculpts a lion
from Aegean sand, like a chemist

trying to calculate the formula for desire.
Each day she feeds her lion
octopus & chickpeas, waiting for

him to break out in hives.
But he only grows stronger, harder,
more measured in his movements.

So she braids her hair, plunges into the sea,
discovers a child in an oyster shell.
She knows that soon the North Wind

will start to blow away all the sand
and what will remain is made of marble.

Collects Pebbles

Little stones in her mouth,

instead of teeth. When she opens
to speak, a river of weight falls.

Each small thud blooms into a letter.
As if she could spell some new beginning.

Finds the Sea Cave

Hidden from the shore, she stumbles
over rocks along a goat path

that lead to an opening of sea and fault.
The waves suck salt out of stones,

reach into these fissures, compress
the air. The rock is splintered piece

by piece. She grinds monkey bones,
sprinkling such ends outside of this holy place.

Holds herself up to the swollen sun.
It is time for reaping; but no god

will have this broken sacrifice.
When she enters the sea cave,

sea swirling over cobbles, honey
rains from above, rinses her in light.

Prepares Her Own Nest

Furrowed clouds plow the sky, crossing
paths with asphalt. Trees begin
releasing leaves. She fights the changing

seasons with appropriate ammunition,
knows she must harvest soon, but is afraid
of what she's planted. She hopes

for pumpkins and cold-resistant gourds
to nourish her winter months.
Her history is the struggle

of containment: opening mouth, not
opening mouth, that fracture and fissure
of body and mind. Just the memory

of spring, the splitting of streams,
embrace of roots and ground, a smear of dirt
across her forehead, and also the hesitation

of summer's first green, its promise.
The first bee in the garden charting
its first zig-zag path

from flower to flower. Sweet
pollen. Hers will be a history of release:
the swarm and its queen

looking to nest. A stomach full
of nectar on a warm day. She uproots
trees by hauling their burlap sacks,

sets them between cushions,
bags leaves to fluff her mattress.
She mixes pumpkin seeds with glow paint,

leaves a trail so squirrels can sneak
into the basement at night. Then she brings
the spiders, keeping them

in the bathtub with tomato blossoms
and fruit flies. At last, she shuts the windows,
crawls into her own webbed nest.

CPSIA information can be obtained
at www.ICGtesting.com
Printed in the USA
FFOW04n1702131014
7948FF